LIQUIDATION GOLD

A GUIDE TO BUYING AND SELLING STORE RETURNS AND OVERSTOCK ITEMS ON EBAY

LUKE LANGFORD

Introduction

Why sell liquidation items on eBay?

So, you've thought about selling on eBay but you're not sure what to do. Have you noticed that there are niches amongst the sellers? Some of the sellers with the highest amount of positive feedback seemingly sell just the right things, but how do you know if those things are what you want to sell? There are wholesalers out there that offer big profits and include drop shipping in their services but you don't control the condition of the items, which could lead to a loss of profit when you issue a refund; especially if you have to issue many. The feedback alone could damage your reputation as a seller beyond repair. Being a wholesaler or dropshipper may have its benefits, but your return on investment is a lot smaller than buying liquidation inventory.

Selling liquidated items just may be the avenue into selling on eBay that you're looking for. But why liquidated? Liquidated items are items that have been returned to the store for whatever reason and can't be resold, or overstock items that have gone to clearance and didn't sell when it was time to make space for new product. Manufacturers may not require the item to be returned to them for the seller to get credit. The seller then has to do something with it to free up shelves and hooks for new inventory, so why not re-sell it? Often times, if the seller has received credit for the item from the manufacturer they can then resell it for half of what they paid and still make a profit.

Selling the right liquidation items can be profitable. Here's an example, you buy a lot of designer handbags for twenty-five dollars. Say there are ten in the lot. A Michael Kors (MK) handbag can go for one hundred and thirty-eight dollars (brand new, that's the cheapest on the site) up to thirteen thousand dollars (brand new, most expensive on the site)! If you have just one MK bag with tags and no stains, rips, tears or other defects you can sell it for one hundred dollars and make a profit because you really only paid two dollars and fifty cents per bag in the lot. Now, if you had two MK bags double that. You just made eighty times what you spent on those two bags.

Does that sound good to you? Keep reading to learn more tricks on selling liquidated items on eBay.

Chapter One
In the beginning

Ready to start? Wait! There are a few other things you need to know before you hit the internet in search of your score. One thing to remember is time. Why time? Because, as with any business, time equals money. If you spend too much time scouring the internet you're wasting money. How is that possible? Follow the sites you'll be learning about in chapter three to save yourself time!

First things first. Now that you've made the decision to sell liquidation items on eBay make sure you have an eBay account. If you don't have one it's really easy to set one up.

Accounts

Personal

Go to eBay.com and find the register link in the upper left corner.

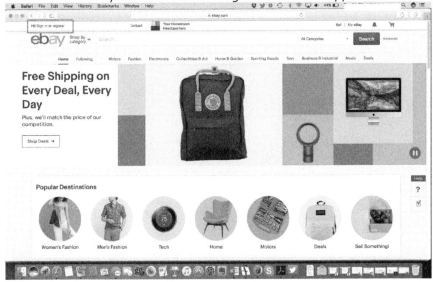

Figure 1. eBay home screen.

Once you've clicked that link you get this:

Figure 2. eBay account creation screen.

Choose if you'd like a business account, or a personal one. If you have a Tax ID Number, are tax exempt, and plan on using this information to run your eBay business please select Business Account. Due to IRS regulations, there will be pertinent information that must be filled out for your business before you can begin selling. However, if you're doing this without all that, please feel free to choose Personal Account (it's free) and follow the following steps to create an account:

1. Fill in the email you want associated with your eBay account. (It's recommended that you keep this separate from your personal email account so that you don't lose emails!)
2. Choose your 6 – 64-character password and it must include at least one number and one special character.
3. You can opt to use a land line if you'd rather not use your cell phone.
4. Enter their Captcha code and the password you want (again because it won't save after you click register, since they want to make sure you're human).
5. Once you click register for the last time, be aware that you're agreeing to their terms and conditions. You're also verifying

that you're over the age of eighteen and can be in a legally binding contract.

Once that's done you'll get another screen:

Figure 3. eBay PIN screen.

Congratulations! You now have an eBay account! Take a look around and get a feel for what is selling so you can make an informed decision on what liquidated items you want to sell.

Seller

Now that you've had the chance to poke around eBay as a buyer (hopefully you've made a purchase or two so you understand that process), let's upgrade you to a Seller's Account. You can do this at any time after you set up your account. It's not unusual to have a buyer's account before your seller's account. Some people just buy, others log in to get rid of some stuff that's been collecting dust on their shelves. No matter what the reason, you'll be in good company.

Let's look at your eBay home screen. To start your seller account, just click Sell.

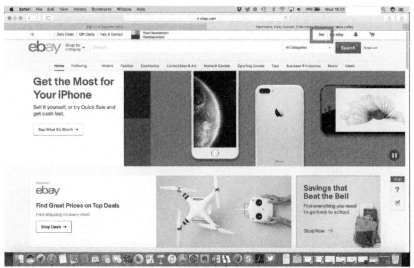

Figure 4. eBay home screen once signed in.

Once you've done that you'll have to add an address. Don't worry, you won't get junk mail from adding it. They require an address for billing.

Figure 5. eBay's add your address screen for all accounts that want to sell.

Once you've got that filled out you're ready to go! You'll not get a confirmation screen per say. What you will get is the "what do you want to sell" screen. Click on "Create a Listing" and happy eBaying!

Business

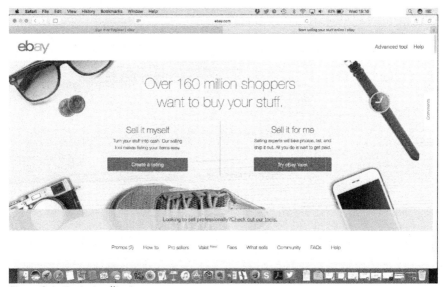

Figure 6. Let's start selling!

Now, let's look at getting you set up with a Business Account. In order to do that you must have an address on file just like the Seller's Account. However, there are a couple of differences. You must have a business name and authorization to create the account.

Figure 7. Creating a business account.

Once you've entered your business information you'll get to choose your Username. You'll notice that as a Personal Account you get assigned a User Name. Click "Save and Continue."

Figure 8. Username set up screen.

This is the step in which you must have a legal address for your business

Figure 9. Business address screen.

When you're done, you will be asked to verify your number. Once that's done, you're set up as a business. The next thing to do is figure out which kind of eBay store you want!

Stores

Before we get into stores let's quickly examine the free, non-store front of a low volume seller. If you're not going to list more than fifty items a month, then stick to the free version. The first fifty items, more often than not, are free! The only time you'll pay a fee is at the end of the auction and it will be based on the end value.

Free-insertion-fee listings

All sellers get free-insertion-fee listings every month.
- Selling limits apply
- Some categories are excluded from free-insertion fees. See excluded categories.

Free-insertion-fee listings each month

	No Store	Basic Store	Premium Store	Anchor Store
Number of free-insertion-fee listings per month	50 fixed price or auction-style listings	250 fixed price listings +250 auction-style listings in select categories	1,000 fixed price listings +500 auction-style listings in select categories	10,000 fixed price listings +1,000 auction-style listings in select categories

Stores free-insertion-fee auction-style listings include the following fashion and collectibles categories:
- Clothing, Shoes & Accessories
- Health & Beauty
- Jewelry & Watches
- Antiques
- Art
- Coins & Paper Money
- Collectibles
- Dolls & Bears
- Entertainment Memorabilia

Figure 10a. eBay's Free insertion fee terms & conditions.

- Toys & Hobbies

listings:
- A calendar month begins at 12:00:00 am Pacific Time on the first day of each month and ends at 11:59:59 pm Pacific Time on the last day of the month.
- Final value fees apply when your item sells.
- Fees for optional advanced listing upgrades and services you may use (such as Bold) still apply.
- If you list in 2 categories, you're charged the regular insertion fee for the second category.
- All categories are eligible for free insertion-fee listings depending on listing style and the insertion fee credit for auction-style listings that end in a sale except:
  - Real Estate
  - The following Motors subcategories: Boats, Cars & Trucks, Motorcycles, Other Vehicles & Trailers, and Powersports.
  - The following Business & Industrial categories
    - Heavy Equipment
    - Concession Trailers & Carts (found in Restaurant & Catering)
    - Imaging & Aesthetics Equipment (found in Healthcare, Lab & Life Science)
    - Commercial Printing Presses (found in Printing & Graphic Arts)
- The following count toward your monthly free-insertion-fee listings:
  - Manual and automatically relisted items
  - The original listing and each renewal for Good 'Til Cancelled listings
  - Listings that you end early, or we end early
  - Duplicate identical auction-style listings (even if one or more of those listings doesn't appear on eBay

Once you've decided how much volume you'll be listing every month you can subscribe to one of the stores and your insertion fees will be lower.

Figure 10b. Free insertion fee continued.

Basic, Premium, or Anchor, which do you choose? It all comes down to your operating budget for the year or the month and if you're confident you'll be rolling in the cash. If you're not a super seller, Anchor may not be for you and

Premium might be the right fit. You can always change your subscription should your needs change.

Before you decide, there are some requirements for each subscription.

Figure 11. Subscription Fees

Recommendations and Requirements

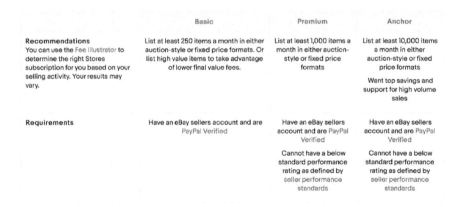

	Basic	Premium	Anchor
Recommendations You can use the Fee Illustrator to determine the right Stores subscription for you based on your selling activity. Your results may vary.	List at least 250 items a month in either auction-style or fixed price formats. Or list high value items to take advantage of lower final value fees.	List at least 1,000 items a month in either auction-style or fixed price formats	List at least 10,000 items a month in either auction-style or fixed price formats Want top savings and support for high volume sales
Requirements	Have an eBay sellers account and are PayPal Verified	Have an eBay sellers account and are PayPal Verified Cannot have a below standard performance rating as defined by seller performance standards	Have an eBay sellers account and are PayPal Verified Cannot have a below standard performance rating as defined by seller performance standards

Figure 12. Recommendations & requirements for eBay stores.

Still want a bit more information? Here's a breakdown comparison of the features of each subscription.

Great Value in Every Stores Subscription Package

Fees	Basic	Premium	Anchor
Monthly subscription	$24.95/month	$74.95/month	$349.95/month
Yearly subscription (1 year term required)	$19.95/month	$59.95/month	$299.95/month
Unlimited insertion fee credits for auction-style listings that end in a sale (exclusions apply†)	✅	✅	✅
Discounted fixed price insertion fee†	20¢	10¢	5¢
Discounted auction-style insertion fee†	25¢	15¢	10¢
Lower final value fees	3.5%-9.15%	3.5%-9.15%	3.5%-9.15%
Number of free fixed price insertion fee listings**†(per month)	250	1,000	10,000
Number of free auction-style insertion fee listings for collectibles and fashion categories only (per month)**	250	500	1,000
Number of free auction-style or fixed price insertion fee listings for guitars and basses category only (per month)**	unlimited	unlimited	unlimited
Benefits	Basic	Premium	Anchor
eBay-branded shipping supplies quarterly coupon***	$25/qtr.	$50/qtr.	$150/qtr.
Promoted listings quarterly credit††	✖	✖	$25/qtr.

Figure 13a. Comparison

	Basic	Premium	Anchor
Additional promoted listings quarterly credit for Top Rated sellers[tt]	$30/qtr.	$30/qtr.	$30/qtr.
Dedicated customer support[tt]	✖	✖	✓
Build your brand	Basic	Premium	Anchor
Store home page *A single, branded place on eBay where all your listings live.*	✓	✓	✓
Customized web address *Get your very own URL (www.stores.ebay.com/yourstorename) so you can drive buyers directly to your Store.*	✓	✓	✓
Featured items *Promote 4 featured items on your Store homepage.*	✓	✓	✓
Store categories *Help buyers browse your Store with 300 custom categories.*	300	300	300
Branding *Add a billboard, logo and description to express your brand, show your products, or announce a promotion or Store event.*	✓	✓	✓
Subscriber discounts *Take advantage of partner discounts on select services to help you manage and grow your business.*	✓	✓	✓
Manage your sales	Basic	Premium	Anchor
Free sales management tools *Use these valuable free tools to help you save time, improve customer satisfaction, and scale your business*	Seller Hub Exclusive Features***	Seller Hub Exclusive Features*** plus Selling Manager Pro (reg. $15.99/month)	Seller Hub Exclusive Features*** plus Selling Manager Pro (reg. $15.99/month)

Figure 13b. Comparison continued.

16

	Basic	Premium	Anchor
Vacation hold *Put your listings and Store "on hold" while you're away.*	✓	✓	✓
Drive traffic	Basic	Premium	Anchor
Exclusive tools to optimize your listings *Take advantage of powerful tools that help boost sales and visibility. (Promotions Manager, Promoted Listings and Markdown Manager)*	✓	✓	✓
On eBay *A link to your eBay Store will appear on all of your listings.*	✓	✓	✓
Listing frame *Add your Store header, search box, and category navigation to all of your listings in your item description.*	✓	✓	✓
HTML builder *Easily create links to your Store from emails, other websites, and listings.*	✓	✓	✓
Off eBay email marketing and promotional emails (per month) *Keep your customers coming back with customized e-newsletters and promotional emails.*	5,000	7,500	10,000
Promotional flyers *Create promotional flyers and include them with your shipments to drive repeat business.*	✓	✓	✓
Business collateral templates *Boost your brand and establish a professional image with these downloadable templates.*	✓	✓	✓
Search engine keyword management *Optimize your Store for search engines and increase your exposure on the web.*	✓	✓	✓

Figure 13c. Comparison continued.

17

Accounting/Bookkeeping

Now that you've decided on your store subscription it's time to get into how you're going to keep the books! It's best if you have a good program rather than trying to do it the old-fashioned way with a ledger. It's always best to research which program will work for you.

Business News Daily[1] has compiled a list of the best small business accounting software and the criteria they used to evaluate each program is what any small business owner should take a look at:
Cost
Ease of use
Time-saving features
Reporting capabilities
Mobile access and mobile features
Account access
Service limitations (number of customers, invoices, users, transactions packages allow)
Customer service
Additional services like credit card processing, tax preparation and payroll services
Integration with third party apps

You've probably heard of their number one pick, QuickBooks Online. Intuit has been a leading retailer for financial software for personal as well as business and they've entered the monthly subscription cloud-based service arena. They offer a wide range of software this way rather than the old three programs available via CD Rom. Who still has a desktop computer or laptop with a CD Rom drive? QuickBooks Online starts at ten dollars for the lowest package. Visit the Intuit QuickBooks to compare and find the best fit for you. A big plus for QuickBooks is that it integrates with PayPal, the preferred payment platform for eBay.

If you're on a shoestring budget that won't allow you to pay per month for cloud software, Business News Daily recommends Wave Accounting. They also offer secure integration with PayPal. You can find

---

[1] *http://www.businessnewsdaily.com/7543-best-accounting-software.html*

Wave Accounting at waveapps.com. Reviewing their website, it seems that this would be best if your business will consist of just you but if you plan on adding more than ten employees to help you sort, catalogue and photograph, or post to your eBay account, then this may not be the software for you. However, it's got the best price tag to start out, free.

Those are both great but what if you're using Mac? Not to worry, Xero is on Business News Daily's list as best software for Mac. Offering three packages, Starter, Standard, and Premium, Xero requires no contract and boasts that clients can cancel service at any time. The company also offers a free thirty-day trial. Should you visit Xero.com you'll see the "Why Xero?" tab. Under that tab, you'll find that the company really knows how to market to different clientele as they have broken down what type of business you'll be using the software for with corresponding information for each category. The only drawback could be the limitations on how many invoices you can send in the first package. Starter only allows five while Standard and Premium allow unlimited invoices and email. If you use QuickBooks and decide that it's not for you Xero offers the ability to convert you QuickBooks files.

What if you don't plan to have added things like employees and payroll? Business News Daily suggests Zoho Books for microbusinesses, which is what your one-person liquidation resale business is. Zoho Books gives you more bang for your buck for the small business option. At twenty-four dollars per month you get customer service twenty-four seven from support centers located in the U.S., the U.K., India, and Australia. Zoho Books does have a "no credit card" fourteen-day free trial. There are cons to this software too. It doesn't integrate with some third-party apps, so be aware of that.

All of these are great choices, however always seek out a free "try before you buy" offer to see if the software you chose with integrate properly and to see if it will be the best fit for your business.

Payments

Now that you've thought about bookkeeping, what about payments? As mentioned previously PayPal is the preferred payment vendor. Whether you choose to accept personal checks or not is up to you. There are some vendors that have never had a problem and there are even more vendors that will swear to never take a personal check again! The caution is strong with this one. If you do decide to take a personal check, always insist to receive the check and it must clear the bank before you ship the items. It is good practice to have a return check fee. Sometimes this is a deterrent to those that willingly pass fraudulent checks. Research processors and fees in your area. You can also request cashier's checks or money orders in lieu of personal checks. Again, with the stipulation that the payment must arrive and clear before you ship.

Most people on eBay these days have a PayPal account. If you don't have one, it's really easy to sign up. Go over to PayPal.com and set up your account. PayPal has two options, Personal and Business. The business account is such that it truly is geared toward the merchant with a website and brick and store. It will not be suitable for your venture into this type of selling on eBay. Choose to set up the personal account and follow these steps:

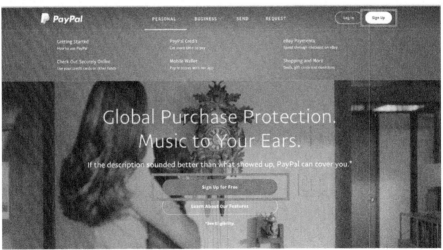

Figure 14. PayPal sign up, two different buttons...same result!

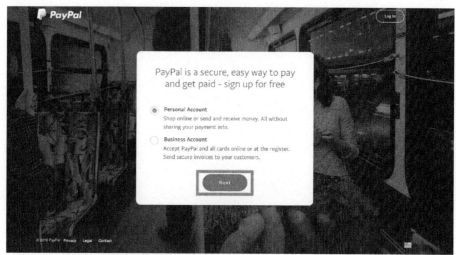

Figure 15. PayPal account type selection... You're on your way to greatness!

Once you've clicked next you'll need to fill out your information and select a password. You'll see this screen:

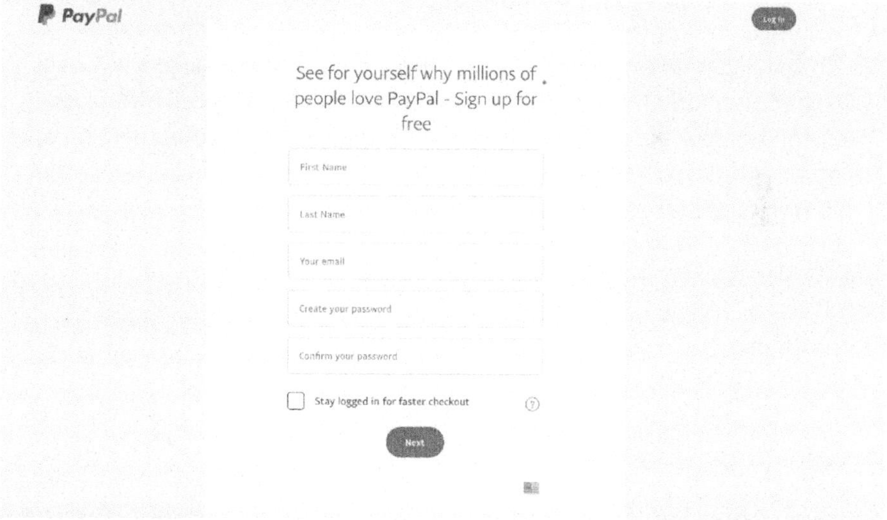

Figure 16. PayPal wants some basics to grant an account.

You have the option to stay logged in. It is completely up to you if you chose to do so. When you continue, you'll get this screen:

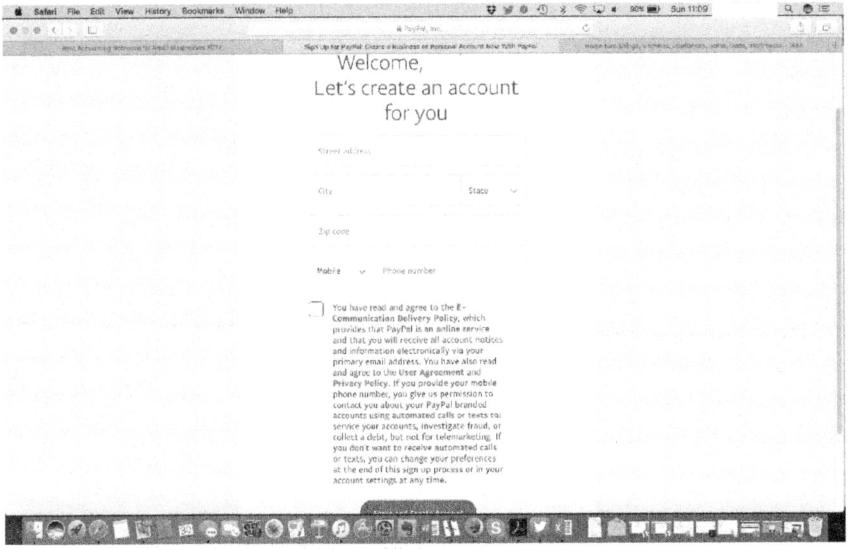

Figure 17. You'll have to agree when you fill this out!

It is recommended that you take the time to read the detail before you check the box and then agree, creating your account. You'll also need a valid phone number. It is helpful to use your cell phone, then you can tie your account to the PayPal mobile app, which is amazing and a great addition to your buying and selling arsenal. Once you've finished this step, you'll get another screen:

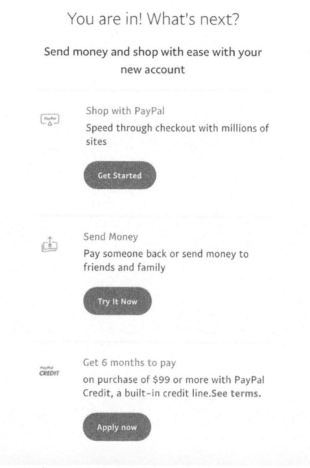

Figure 18. What to do after you have your PayPal account!

You don't have to click any of these in order to get to your PayPal dashboard. In the left-hand corner of this screen there's PayPal logo. Click that and you'll be re-directed to your dashboard where you can do anything you need to set up your account. Now, in order to be a seller on eBay with whatever option you chose you must be verified. In order to do that you must add a bank account. Here's where the other part of bookkeeping comes in. It is highly recommended that you have a separate bank account for your business. You don't, necessarily, have to have a Tax Identification Number (TIN) to open the account if you stick to a non-business account. If you chose to open a business account with your local financial institution you will be required to have a TIN from the IRS, if you're in the U.S. Residents of countries outside the U.S. must inquire with their local governments what is required to start a business. You may also link a credit card but that will not verify you as a seller.

Congratulations! You now have a PayPal account! PayPal has a majority of the tools you will need to keep your eBay business running.

If you're still not sure about bookkeeping, you can hire someone to help you or you can Google a nearby college or university and take an introduction to business course. You may even be able to find a college student that is working on their degree in business willing to tutor you. It never hurts to inquire.

Office Space or Garage Storage?

The next bit of the business is to have somewhere to test and store your merchandise. It's helpful if you have a garage big enough, especially if you're buying pallets full, that is the ideal place to store your inventory. The key to being successful is to keep your stock organized, like items together.

To keep yourself organized, use shelving units, bins and labels. Ikea and The Container Store are good options to find storage solutions. Any big box home improvement store will also have storage solutions that will also fit your needs. It comes down to what you have in your area. It doesn't need to be fancy but if you have to store items in a garage you may want to hang Damp-Rid bags to protect your inventory from moisture and store it on a shelving unit with doors.

Same principles apply if you have a spare room in your home that you plan on using to store you stock but you don't need to have doors on the shelving unit, unless you have a curious pet that likes to investigate new things. When selling on eBay it's best to make sure that you annotate in your listing if your item comes from a pet-free, or pet-friendly home, but more about listings later!

You may want to set up a home office complete with your computer, merchandise, camera, an area set up for photographing your stock, and your shipping supplies. This keeps everything in one place for easy access. It really does come down to what space you have available for your business.

Whatever you sell, you'll need some space to test the items. Especially, important if you're selling electronics or toys that move (like R.C. vehicles). You want to inspect every product that comes into your business. It should be in working order to sell it. Testing will be in a chapter later!

Supplies

You'll need to stock up on boxes. You can get a wide range of sizes from Uline.com or if you chose to offer USPS Priority Mail as an option for shipping you can acquire those boxes for free from the post office. For smaller items, bubble mailers can save you a ton of money in shipping costs. Just make sure that if there is even a slight chance that the item could break during shipping, bubble wrap the heck out of it or put it in a box. Also, make sure you save any boxes that have been sent to you from your own purchases. You'll also want to invest in a scale to weigh your items. To calculate your shipping after you've photographed your item, box it up with your packing material and set it on your scale to get an accurate weight. Shippers, no matter the service you choose, will weigh the box and contents, not just the item itself. There have been instances (in the beginning there is always a learning curve) of not charging enough for shipping and that eats into the profits you earned on the item.

A Dymo LabelWriter 450 Twin Turbo is recommended if you need to print two different size labels. The software runs on either PC or Mac and is one of the more popular label printers. If you want to keep your labels separate, you can pick up a Zebra printer for shipping labels, a wide range can be purchased from Uline.com. Zebra printers are designed for shipping labels. If you can't afford one of those yet, your home printer can be used and shipping labels can be purchased from your local office supply store.

eBay has a partnership with the USPS that allows eBay sellers a bit of a discount on their shipping. You can also print your shipping labels right from eBay and have the price of the shipping taken from your PayPal account. It's really convenient and quick to do without the extra cost of the Dymo and Zebra printers if they aren't in your budget right now.

Uline is a company geared toward businesses. They sell a lot of great shipping supplies in bulk at reasonable prices as well as a wide variety of other business items you may discover you need. They also sell display, shelving, and storage solutions. Check them out if Ikea, The Container Store, or home improvement places don't meet your needs.

The most important supply you need to have and will make or break your listing is a camera. If you don't have a big budget to start, a cellphone camera, a photography box and really good lighting will do. Make sure your camera on your phone takes really good quality pictures. Be sure that you can expand the memory on your phone. (iPhones do not have this ability but a majority of Android platform phones do!) You'll be taking a lot of pictures and without an additional memory card you'll fill up the phone memory fast.

A favorite camera that is easy to use is the Samsung WB350F. It's a few years old and no longer available new, however you can find it used. The biggest advantage is that you can plug it into your computer and upload all of the images at once to eBay. It takes great close ups and it auto focuses. If you do have room in your start-up budget for a camera go ahead and invest in a DSLR or a small point and shoot. Keep in mind that you'll want to be able to upload multiple images when you plug it in, or if your computer has a card reader slot, you'll want to be able to upload your images from the memory card. Do your research

Photography light boxes give you a good space to shoot small to medium size items. They tend to block out excess light from the sides as well. Google them and you can find a wide variety, including instructions on building your own. If you use a backdrop, you want a solid color. Grays and blacks are good. Blues have been used but it really depends on the color of the product you're going to be shooting. You don't want a dark color against a dark color or light against light. If you're not sure how to best capture the best pictures do a little research, or when you purchase your camera ask for one on one classes. (This option is most often available if you purchase from a specialty camera store rather than a big box electronics retailer.)

Remember, if you are serious about making this a business, you need the proper tools to succeed. A quality camera will help sell items, prevent customers from asking for more pics because they can't zoom in and see the details, and make listing items faster.

Chapter Two
So, you've got a store. Now what?

Research

Research is an important part of learning about the products you're going to be selling. As soon as your designer handbags arrive inventory, catalog, and inspect them. Then, sit down at the computer and research each designer as well as their products. After that's done, research the specific bag you have to sell. That way if you have to answer any questions about the item you can sound like you know exactly what you're talking about because you will know! You probably research the newest gadgets before you purchase one, treat this the same. You'll want to give your buyers the confidence that buying from you will be the best experience they have on eBay and knowing your products is one way to do that.

Part of your research should include the original pricing of the bag, what other sellers are selling it for, and what can you afford to sell it for to make a profit and not be stuck with something no one is buying. Be mindful that you shouldn't go by the retail value on the manifest. Now, designer bags are just an example. This applies to any kind of product you will be selling not just handbags.

Most of your purchases are in boxes or pallets with an assortment of items. Just make sure you look up the pricing and potential sell-through of all of the items prior to bidding on the lot

Ten Percent Rule to Maximize Profit

When bidding on an auction, if you use the ten percent rule, your chances of taking a loss severely decrease. If you can recoup your investment in ten percent of the items in the lot, then the rest becomes your profit. For example, if you buy a lot on liquidation.com that has forty-four items it in and you paid two hundred dollars, you should be able to recoup your investment with four or five items. One reason this method is effective: they always "pad" the manifest with several low value items. Most of those items still have a value, but you can't count on those items. Also, if you purchase the lot because you think the most expensive item in the lot will make you a ton of money, what happens if it arrives broken, missing, or incomplete?

Figures 19a and 19b show a recently purchased lot, forty-four items for two hundred and four dollars after shipping. When bidding it was determined that after the first five items in the lot (highlighted in 19b) the investment could be recouped. After the lot was received, tested, listed and everything sold, the lot produced over six hundred dollars in profit after fees.

Product	Quantity	Retail Price	Total Retail Price	UPC	Notes
MiP Exclusive Deluxe Pack - White	1	$138.10	$138.10	771171128212	
Riviera RC Ninco Air Quadrone with Nano Cam	1	$135.99	$135.99	609722357401	
BLADE Nano QX RTF Quadcopter	1	$79.99	$79.99	605482096352	
BLADE Nano QX RTF Quadcopter	1	$79.99	$79.99	605482096352	
SYMA X5C-W 4CH 2.4G Quadcopter with Camera	1	$63.99	$63.99	844949021678	
SYMA X5C-W 4CH 2.4G Quadcopter with Camera	1	$63.99	$63.99	844949021678	
SYMA X5C-W 4CH 2.4G Quadcopter with Camera	1	$63.99	$63.99	844949021678	
SYMA X5C-W 4CH 2.4G Quadcopter with Camera	1	$63.99	$63.99	844949021678	
SYMA X5C-W 4CH 2.4G Quadcopter with Camera	1	$63.99	$63.99	844949021678	
SYMA X5C-W 4CH 2.4G Quadcopter with Camera	1	$63.99	$63.99	844949021678	
SYMA X5C-W 4CH 2.4G Quadcopter with Camera	1	$63.99	$63.99	844949021678	
SYMA X5C-W 4CH 2.4G Quadcopter with Camera	1	$63.99	$63.99	844949021678	
SYMA X5C-W 4CH 2.4G Quadcopter with Camera	1	$63.99	$63.99	844949021678	
Nano QX BNF with SAFE	1	$62.65	$62.65		
UDI RC U27 3D Inverted Flight Drone	1	$33.46	$33.46	844949026215	
UDI RC U27 3D Inverted Flight Drone	1	$33.46	$33.46	844949026215	
UDI RC U27 3D Inverted Flight Drone	1	$33.46	$33.46	844949026215	
UDI RC U27 3D Inverted Flight Drone	1	$33.46	$33.46	844949026215	
UDI RC U27 3D Inverted Flight Drone	1	$33.46	$33.46	844949026215	
UDI RC U27 3D Inverted Flight Drone	1	$33.46	$33.46	844949026215	
Udirc Venom UDI001-O 2.4GHz High Speed Remote Control Electric Boat (Orange)	1	$32.29	$32.29	724716438444	
Udirc Venom UDI001-O 2.4GHz High Speed Remote Control Electric Boat (Orange)	1	$32.29	$32.29	724716438444	
Air Hogs Altitude Video Drone	1	$30.55	$30.55	795545903175	
Air Hogs Altitude Video Drone	1	$30.55	$30.55	795545903175	
Air Hogs Altitude Video Drone	1	$30.55	$30.55	795545903175	
Syma X11 R/C Quadcopter - White	1	$29.99	$29.99		
Estes Proto X Nano R/C Quadcopter, Purple	1	$29.54	$29.54	047776047082	
Syma X11 R/C Quadcopter - Red	1	$28.78	$28.78		
Syma X11 R/C Quadcopter - Red	1	$28.78	$28.78		
Syma X11 R/C Quadcopter - Red	1	$28.78	$28.78		

Figure 19a. Sample Manifest

Product	Quantity	Retail Price	Total Retail Price	UPC	Notes
MiP Exclusive Deluxe Pack - White	1	$138.10	$138.10	771171128212	
Riviera RC Ninco Air Quadrone with Nano Cam	1	$135.99	$135.99	609722357401	
BLADE Nano QX RTF Quadcopter	1	$79.99	$79.99	605482096352	
BLADE Nano QX RTF Quadcopter	1	$79.99	$79.99	605482096352	
SYMA X5C-W 4CH 2.4G Quadcopter with Camera	1	$63.99	$63.99	844949021678	
SYMA X5C-W 4CH 2.4G Quadcopter with Camera	1	$63.99	$63.99	844949021678	
SYMA X5C-W 4CH 2.4G Quadcopter with Camera	1	$63.99	$63.99	844949021678	
SYMA X5C-W 4CH 2.4G Quadcopter with Camera	1	$63.99	$63.99	844949021678	
SYMA X5C-W 4CH 2.4G Quadcopter with Camera	1	$63.99	$63.99	844949021678	
SYMA X5C-W 4CH 2.4G Quadcopter with Camera	1	$63.99	$63.99	844949021678	
SYMA X5C-W 4CH 2.4G Quadcopter with Camera	1	$63.99	$63.99	844949021678	
SYMA X5C-W 4CH 2.4G Quadcopter with Camera	1	$63.99	$63.99	844949021678	
SYMA X5C-W 4CH 2.4G Quadcopter with Camera	1	$63.99	$63.99	844949021678	
Nano QX BNF with SAFE	1	$62.65	$62.65		
UDI RC U27 3D Inverted Flight Drone	1	$33.46	$33.46	844949026215	
UDI RC U27 3D Inverted Flight Drone	1	$33.46	$33.46	844949026215	
UDI RC U27 3D Inverted Flight Drone	1	$33.46	$33.46	844949026215	
UDI RC U27 3D Inverted Flight Drone	1	$33.46	$33.46	844949026215	
UDI RC U27 3D Inverted Flight Drone	1	$33.46	$33.46	844949026215	
UDI RC U27 3D Inverted Flight Drone	1	$33.46	$33.46	844949026215	
Udirc Venom UDI001-O 2.4GHz High Speed Remote Control Electric Boat (Orange)	1	$32.29	$32.29	724716438444	
Udirc Venom UDI001-O 2.4GHz High Speed Remote Control Electric Boat (Orange)	1	$32.29	$32.29	724716438444	
Air Hogs Altitude Video Drone	1	$30.55	$30.55	795545903175	
Air Hogs Altitude Video Drone	1	$30.55	$30.55	795545903175	
Air Hogs Altitude Video Drone	1	$30.55	$30.55	795545903175	
Syma X11 R/C Quadcopter - White	1	$29.99	$29.99		
Estes Proto X Nano R/C Quadcopter, Purple	1	$29.54	$29.54	047776047082	
Syma X11 R/C Quadcopter - Red	1	$28.78	$28.78		
Syma X11 R/C Quadcopter - Red	1	$28.78	$28.78		
Syma X11 R/C Quadcopter - Red	1	$28.78	$28.78		

Figure 19b. Sample Manifest

Chapter Three
Where's the merch?

Now that you've got a store on eBay, a PayPal account, your business space set up, and an idea of how you're going to track your income, you need product! This brief chapter will give you the lowdown on some picks. As always, you'll want to research which site is the best for you and your needs. You can always change or upgrade later as your growing budget allows!

Liquidation.com
Bulq.com
Bstocksupply.com
Techliquidators.com
Boxfox.co
Wholesalecentral.com

You can Google "wholesale liquidation lots" and come up with more if this list doesn't meet your needs. A word of caution, do your due diligence in research and make sure any sites you find are legitimate wholesalers and research the manifests thoroughly before purchasing.

Liquidation.com – You must bid on the lots that you're interested in. They offer shipping or pick up if the location is local to you. They also source from Amazon Liquidations, but it's not limited to Amazon. It's free to sign up. (Amazon is currently Beta testing a liquidation section to their own site. However, it appears that it will be strictly for business customers.) This is one of the best sites. You can purchase lots for ten to fifteen percent of retail cost and most of the time, customer return goods are in great condition and sometimes new. Just make sure when you are bidding, you use the ten percent rule because sometimes the items do still arrive broken, not working, or missing parts. Also, the auction sizes are smaller and more affordable. If you are bidding on a lot, just put your max bid price in and let them increase the bids for you. Many people get into the thrill of bidding live and will bid much higher than their profit margins allow. It's fun while you are bidding, but can be brutal to your profit margins. Remember, if you don't win this auction, there are hundreds more that day.

Bulq.com – Free to create an account. They have a manifest that is downloadable (an Excel file) and has all the information you'll need for each lot. They tell you were the lot came from like Home Goods or Gramercy. A big plus is no bidding. You can add the lot to your cart. This site is also nice because they presort and test the items before listing. Just because they didn't find a defect, doesn't mean it's not there though. Sometimes you pay a higher premium for their lots, but you have a better chance of knowing the condition before testing them yourself.

Bstocksupply.com – Another bid site. They are upfront with charging a ten percent final bid value buyer's fee. You also should have a B-Stock Network account to log in and you have to be approved to participate. This is another one of our favorites because they have a large assortment of auctions. One thing to remember about BStock is that payment is by wire transfer only. When you are bidding, look at the seller details, it will show you if buyers have rebought from the seller. That's usually a good indication if they have quality product and descriptions.

Techliquidators.com – (A Best Buy Brand) This site requires a business name and TIN to register for an account. They have a lot of great auctions but be very careful as they have other sellers too. Auction prices are typically high and customer return goods have a higher fallout. Just bid using the ten percent rule here and you'll be ok.

Boxfox.co – This site is free to create an account. They use Stripe and it is a requirement to use their site. There's no way to see an actual listing without signing up for their site. They have a section of their site called Retail University if you need to learn about the retail world. They are also a bidding site. Upside, there's a five percent transaction fee. This site is one of the newer liquidation sites but they are growing fast. Make sure you do you research on the items because more often than not, they are being sold by retailers that are having a hard time moving their products.

Wholesalecentral.com –This is a list of retailers, wholesalers, and other liquidators searching for buyers. You can search by category to find what you're looking for and the list is large! At the bottom of the home page there are other links that are owned by this site. They could be worth checking out.

Chapter Four
Tests? What tests?

We've talked about a few things that are important but this chapter is all about testing! Why testing? Everyone's one hundred percent honest about the condition of items, right? No! When you're buying returned items it's important to check the manifest for any notes on each product. Some sites add notes, others don't. It's up to you to check your manifest. It's best if you can have the manifest in your hands when your lot arrives instead of having to hunt for it in the box. (Most of the time, they don't even include a manifest.) If you buy pallets, more often than not it will be secured in a clear envelope on the outside of the wrap that's marked "Shipping List Enclosed" or "Packing Slip Inside." When you're inventorying your product it's a good idea to check things off in pencil in the event that you make a mistake and need to correct it.

Make sure your manifest has everything listed that's on the pallet or in the box. Be sure to slap a label on everything and match descriptions. Your manifests will help with this. You may get two identical items from different sources with completely different descriptions. Your research will come in handy here so you'll know which description is correct. This will help with listing later! Sometimes, you'll find that you're missing some items. First thing you should do is take pictures of EVERYTHING and document what's missing. Contact the site you purchased from and request a credit for the difference of the missing items. They'll typically try to issue a credit based on the quantity ratio. For example, if you were expecting one hundred items and only received eighty-five, they'll usually suggest a fifteen percent refund. However, if the fifteen items missing were the most expensive items on the manifest, that wouldn't be a fair refund. In that scenario, make sure they base the refund off of the retail value of the manifest. For example, if the manifest retail value was two thousand dollars and you paid one hundred and the missing inventory retail value was five hundred, you should receive a twenty-five percent refund or twenty-five dollars.

Now that everything is inventoried you'll want to inspect and test every item before you put them in their proper place. It's important to ensure electronics work and don't need repair. If you come across say an iPad that is perfect outside but it doesn't power on or stay on after being charged, you can still sell it but you have to make sure that the buyer knows that it's for parts only. You need to be detailed in your descriptions when you list and the testing phase is a perfect time to take notes.

Make sure that everything is in the package that is supposed to be in the package. With some open box laptop returns (like from Best Buy) there may be a missing power cord or manual. Chances of selling a brand new open box laptop without a power cord aren't all that great. Take the extra time to purchase one and note in the listing that it isn't the original power cord but it is compatible. Same goes with an electronics manual. If you can locate one, great! If not, find it online and print it out to include. If not? Again, annotate that in the listing. Make sure you do your research, if the laptop value only changes by ten dollars because it's missing the charger, there is no need to buy a charger for twenty dollars to sell it. If your item is missing a manual, an easy way to describe that is just say the manual is missing but can be found online at the manufacturer website.

When you test a product, go ahead and create the listing on eBay. This will help keep you more organized and will help you remember the small details about the item.

If you have clothes, make sure there are no holes, missing buttons, or seams that have come undone. Sometimes clothes are the easiest things to fix. Missing button and no spare? Go to the local JoAnn Fabric and find buttons that are as close as possible or compliment the fabric and replace all of them. If sewing on buttons is a skill you have, if not it is pretty easy to learn. You can usually find a local seamstress (try looking at your dry cleaner) to repair a hem or a popped seam. It's better in the long run to not re-sell any clothes that are damaged if you can help it.

All of this advice and stress on testing or inspecting your product helps to head off negative feedback. Negative feedback can be overcome but it's hard to do if you have it piled on, so it's best to avoid it all together.

Bottom line? TEST EVERYTHING even if it looks perfect.

Chapter Five

Let's create that listing, shall we?

Now it's time to venture into the waters of selling. You're going to create your very first eBay listing.

To save yourself some time, in your Seller Hub there's a link for "Listing Templates" go ahead a create a few so you have them.

Figure 20. Example of the eBay Seller Hub and Template location.

If you don't want to create them right now, that's fine because you can come back to them at any time. You don't have to use them at all if you aren't inclined to do so. For right now, click on the "Overview" tab. Over on the far right there happens to be a "Listings" section. You can click on "Create Listing."

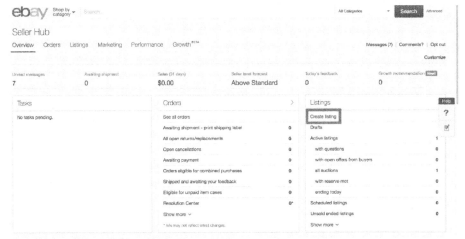

Figure 21. The Overview tab of eBay's Seller Hub

Once you click on that link it will take you to another screen where you'll be able to enter the UPC, ISBN or other description to find your item. In Figure 20 you'll notice an item that was located via UPC because the item was new with tag. The pattern was the only thing that was added to make it easier for someone to locate if they are searching for that particular pattern. If you end up using the eBay app to list (as the item in Figure 20 was) you'll be able to scan the UPC rather than typing it in. You can always log in to your account from your PC and edit items up until there is a bid placed. After bids are placed that's it! No further edits are allowed. If you have questions on the product there's an option to add them to your listing for other buyers to read.

36

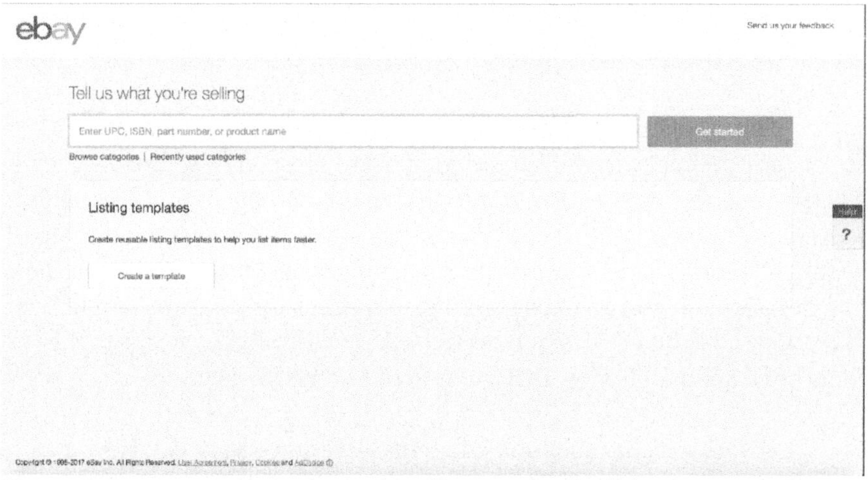

Figure 22. eBay wants to know what you're selling... go ahead, tell them!

Once you've got your listing started, assuming eBay's system found the UPC you've entered, you'll get this:

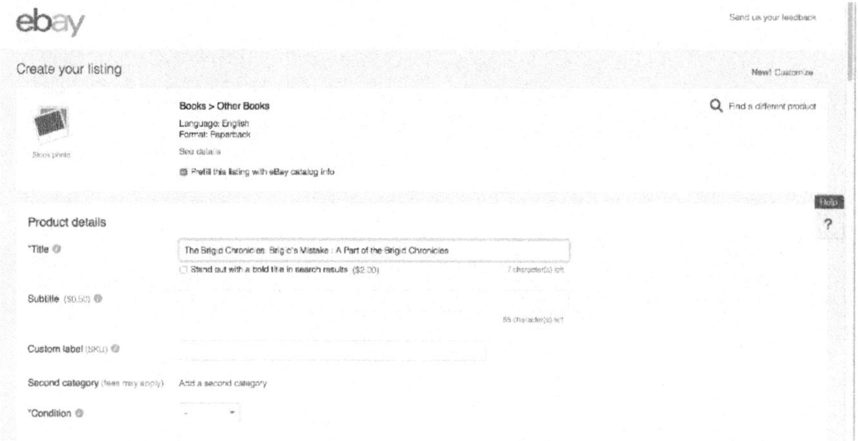

Figure 23. Product details

Scroll down and complete all the information. If you have a custom label with your own SKU number (used for inventory tracking purposes) enter it when you're filling out your info. The next thing you need to know is the condition. eBay has their list of conditions and it's very specific:

New
Like New
Very Good

Good
Acceptable

Pay specific attention to the condition and description. Be as honest as possible with the condition. If there's a scuff or scrape annotate it in the description. Mention which picture the damage is in. Never put an item up as NEW if it has any type of damage. That opens the door for negative feedback and complaints. You can also put the condition in the title of your listing if you chose but it's not necessary unless it Mint In Box (MIB), Out Of Print (OOP), or hard to find. Since you're buying lots the chances of anything being OOP or hard to find will be slim.

Conditions: (Be sure you know the difference between New and Like New, etcetera.)

NEW: Perfect, factory sealed packaging meaning no split plastic or box, factory tape is intact. Never use this unless it meets the perfect criteria.

LIKE NEW: Open Box items. If you've ever purchased open box from Best Buy or another electronics retailer you know what this means, but here's a brief refresher. Something is missing from the package and the original retailer can't sell it or the packaging is damaged. The item was returned for some reason, is in working order but has, say a power cord missing or a manual. Make sure you are very descriptive when you list. If there was a warranty with it and you can't honor that manufacturer's warranty state it clearly (bold font is acceptable to stress this point). List what's there and what is missing.

VERY GOOD: If the item has a few scratches but is obviously not brand new. Again, be descriptive of where the damage is.

GOOD: More than its fair share of wear and tear but still sellable. Annotate, annotate, annotate any and all damage. The more detailed you can be the better and the less questions you have to answer. This is also where good lighting for your photos comes in handy.

ACCEPTABLE: It's obvious that the item has seen better days but it still functions to standard. It's really important with these items that you are as specific as possible with damage. If the corner of the case is cracked but it still functions, someone out there will buy it for ten or twenty bucks instead of buying it brand new for ten times as much.

If the item kind of functions but doesn't fit the previous categories, list as acceptable but put FOR PARTS OR REPAIR ONLY, or some variation since you only have eighty characters, in the title or the very first line in the description. Note if it gets power but doesn't switch on or if there's no power. If you have a volt meter and know how to properly use it you should be able to tell if something with no power is capable of receiving or transferring a current. You may have to field a question on this and you want to be prepared.

Next is the description. Pretty self-explanatory and if you hadn't noticed it is emphasized repeatedly throughout this book. If you fail to leave something out of the description and a buyer says, "Hey, this is jacked up. If I had known I wouldn't have bought it!" You can reply with, "But it says in the description that it was for parts only." eBay has a good buyer protection program as well as a stout seller protection program. They want people to buy and sell their stuff through their site and unhappy people will go to Deal Dash, uBid, or QuiBids. So, it's better to just avoid negative feedback by being up front. However, there will always be that one buyer that insists on a refund.

If you'd like to save time (or if you think your power of description isn't up to snuff) you can search for a matching item to the one you're selling. Find another seller's description and copy and paste. Once you've copied your description, click the "Sell Yours" button and paste your description. A word of warning though, make sure there are no spelling or grammatical errors. If you're not sure, there's a site called Grammarly that allows you to download a plugin for your browser and will scan whatever you write in a text field for errors. The plugin is free and works for the internet. Another note... if you're selling something for "Parts or Repair" be certain that you write your own description of that item.

Refunds? eBay does that? No, you do that. You can offer thirty-day returns with refund and free shipping. To keep from eating your profits up, try limiting the free shipping to weights one pound or less. If you feel the need to offer free shipping to all, add that into the starting price of the auction. Anything over one pound use calculated shipping. This is why you have your item packed and weighed after you photograph it. Some sellers find it helpful to write the shipping weight on the inside flap since it won't be sealed up until the auction is complete.

Do you have to sell auction-style? You sure don't! You can sell fixed price which is great if you have more than one of an item. Say you have a lot of drones with camera that you want to sell at thirty bucks a piece and they are all the same color, condition, and size. It's easier to list them fixed price with a quantity of five or ten. You can also do a private listing so all buyers are anonymous.

A new addition to eBay's Seller Hub listings is sales tax. You should include this according to your location's tax laws. Google your state's secretary of state or revenue office for more information. Some states require that you add sales tax to shipping and handling. eBay has the option to do this.

Did you know that now you can donate a portion of your profits to the charity of your choice? Say you've got a lot that includes some Breast Cancer Awareness items, you can choose to donate to the cancer research organization of your choice a portion of your profit from that item, or all of your profit if you're feeling particularly charitable.

Shipping

Shipping is really important. Sometimes buyers look specifically at items with free shipping. Especially if there are other sellers that have the same item. If you happen to have a slightly higher price but free shipping that buyer may chose you rather than taking the chance of spending twelve bucks on shipping. For this section of the listing you'll need to know the dimensions of the package you're shipping the item in if you're not using the USPS and their flat rate boxes. It also gives the option to ship internationally. This is up to you if you want to do so. With the eBay Global Shipping Program, it's easier than before to ship across the globe. When you purchase the shipping, it will be directed to a hub in the U.S. and eBay's employees take it from there. They handle the customs forms and everything relating to getting it to your overseas customer.

It's advisable to have insurance on the higher dollar items. The USPS Priority Mail offers tracking and up to fifty dollars' insurance. You can opt for a higher amount if the value to replace the item would cost more for an additional fee. If you elect to send parcel post you must purchase additional services like delivery confirmation, signature delivery, and insurance. Having delivery confirmation, even going as far as requiring a signature, will help with fraudulent buyers that claim to never receive your shipment. If they had to sign for it, that information is available when a claim is filed.

Remember, when you package your item to ship, if it had original packaging, be sure that the item is secure in it and pack with packing peanuts (packing popcorn) or bubble wrap to ensure that it arrives in one piece. If something arrives broken and you have to replace it, you lose profits. So, it's better to pack everything well and in the appropriate size boxes than lose money. Use clear packaging tape to seal the box. You want to be sure that water won't get under the flaps of the box, so sealing the edges isn't out of order. After all, anything you have to replace is a loss of profit! Don't use cheap boxes either. Get good shipping boxes. Check out Uline.com, as mentioned before, they have a ton of shipping supplies that are marketed just for retailers.

Labels and more labels! There are so many to choose from. eBay has its own internal postage system powered by Pitney Bowes. It's a decent one and will work for you if you don't invest in a specialty printer. You can pick up shipping labels for a home printer at any office supply store. Just a note of caution, should you use this label system, do not tape over any bar codes! The clear packaging tape interferes with the scanners. If you did go with the Zebra printer or they Dymo 450 Twin Turbo, follow the instructions included in the manual for their respective software.

You've got a mountain of boxes; how do you get them to the post office? Well, whatever shipping service you chose to use has the "schedule a pick up" option. You may have to go to that service's website to schedule but it takes the hassle out of making sure everything gets into the car to go. A word of advice, try sticking to one company. You and your route driver will get to be familiar faces to each other! A plus if you like making new acquaintances but can't get out because you're so busy selling and making mad cash!

One last thing on shipping... include the packing slip. Keep a copy for your records and write the tracking number on it. Enclose a copy for your buyer. As an extra little something, include a handwritten note on the packing slip thanking them for their business. It shows them that you are grateful for the business and that you took the time to inspect the package before shipping it out. This is great when you first get started to help increase your chances for positive feedback. When you start growing and are shipping fifty plus items a day, you may want to buy some cheap business cards that say thank you and your contact information if there are issues. (You can buy Avery 8877 Two-Side Printable White Matte Clean Edge Business Cards and print some on your home printer. They are awesome and easy to break apart.)

When it comes right down to it, everything in your lot is worth something to somebody. If you receive an old cd player that is broken, check the prices on the power adapter, it may be worth just as much as the stereo if it's working. Don't dismiss something because you think it won't sell. List it anyway. Some profit is better than no profit! A perfect example is the show American Pickers on History Channel. They "pick" antiques and try to keep prices they pay down so they have room for profit. Sometimes, if they find a really rare piece they'll pay more and decrease their profit margin to get that item. They know that they have to do that sometimes to keep their customers coming back.

Chapter Six
Help! What's Marketing and Sales?

Running Sales on eBay

Wait. You can run sales on eBay? Why yes, you can. Using the Markdown Manager makes it really easy! You can run a set percentage off your products for a set period of time. (This feature is available to Stores only not individuals.) Try running sales for a short period. The kids these days are calling them flash sales. Flash sales usually run about four to six hours and you'll have to be on top of the listings you run on sale. This may be more helpful if you have someone that can watch your listing for you while you continue

You can also run the sales for a day or two. It helps boost sales at the beginning of the sale as well as the end of the sale. Why would this work to boost sales? eBay sends out notices to the "watchers" letting them know there was a price drop. Toward the end of the sale there is a countdown. It's helpful to do this just for a day or two, especially if you have merchandise that needs to move. Another helpful tip, run a sale back to back to thin out your inventory.

Marketing on eBay

Here's where your Premium Storefront will come in handy. eBay gives you thirty dollars' worth of marketing every ninety days. It's helpful to run a marketing campaign when you have a large quantity of one item. (Example, your lot has dozens of fancy fidget spinners!) You can also run a marketing campaign on a specific category if you have a shipment with a large number of items in that category. (Example, home automation items.) When running marketing campaigns, you have the option to give eBay one to twenty percent of the sale. The plus side of the eBay marketing campaign? You only pay if the item sells. Have you seen the "sponsored" or "promoted" content at the top of your searches when cruising eBay? That's from an eBay marketing campaign.

Chapter Seven
Negative Feedback, Fraudulent Transactions & Bad Buyers, oh my!

Feedback induced anxiety? No worries!

The dreaded negative feedback! Everyone gets that one buyer that no matter what you do will never be happy with the solutions you've offered until they have their money back and your product. These are the people that will end up leaving the negative feedback.

But... how do you combat that negative feedback? When a buyer contacts you with a problem, be courteous. How can you head off negative feedback before it happens? When you list your items be as detailed as possible. Try thinking of every possible question a buyer might ask. If you think you've got all the information, ask someone you trust to read over your description. If they have questions, add that to your listing. It takes time but it's better to get everything out up front and not run the risk of negative feedback.

What happens if you do get negative feedback? It's okay. You'll live as long as you did everything in your power to make the customer happy. What will damage your business? LOTS of negative feedback. Remember, be courteous, keep records of all communications (never communicate outside of the eBay messaging system for this reason, if it's not written down it didn't happen) and smile. There's always someone out there having a worse time of things than you!

If you think that a buyer has violated eBay's feedback policies, don't be afraid to call eBay. What's the worst they could say? They won't remove it?

Returns

The dreaded return. It's a part of owning a retail business, but it's up to you how to handle them. Accepting returns is a loss of profit, however you can control how much gets returned. The key? Being as detailed as possible in your descriptions. That's why it's recommended to have someone else read your descriptions. Sometimes another set of eyes will help you catch the errors in your post before you list and another brain to think of questions you haven't answered yet!

Another handy thing you can do with eBay is setup return shipping rules to automatically accept returns for items that are defective or not as described and provide eBay shipping labels.

Items Not Received

This is tricky. Also, why you should have some form of delivery confirmation and insurance. There are folks out there that want what you're selling but don't want to pay for it, so they buy it and claim that it never arrived; yet when you check the package status it says delivered. Sometimes this situation is unavoidable. If a buyer contacts you with this situation, investigate with whomever you shipped with. Be sure to get eBay involved as necessary. They want everyone to come back to their site, so they will do what they are legally able to do. Usually, if you track down the shipping records and can show that it was delivered it's better to refute the non-received claim. Insurance. Insurance. Insurance! There can't be enough stress on requiring insurance, especially for your big-ticket items. It covers you as well as your buyer.

Every item you sell should be shipped with a tracking number. If a customer claims the item wasn't received and has opened a claim with eBay, you can take a screenshot of the tracking number on the shipping carrier's website showing it was delivered, then contact eBay and they will request a screenshot be uploaded to them. In most cases, you are then protected under the eBay Seller Protection and eBay will close the case in your favor (then the customer can't leave negative feedback).

Bad Buyers

Bad buyers can come from all over. One thing you can do to protect against them is to set your PayPal account to only accept U.S. customers, then you can turn off international shipping. If you don't want to cut your buying pool down to just U.S. buyers, you can use eBay's Global Shipping Program. As mentioned in a previous chapter, you ship your product to an eBay hub and they handle the rest. Whatever you decide to do, there will be one bad buyer that slips through and that's the nature of business.

Chapter Eight
Software? We don't need no stinkin' software!

Shipping

Wait, wait, wait! You may change your mind about software when you hear about ShippingEasy. It's easier when processing several packages a day. You can create a scan sheet to give to the post office so they don't have to scan every package. (eBay does have this option if you do bulk shipping. However, bulk shipping ins eBay is cumbersome and you have to do all the shipping at once.) It may be helpful for you to pick a time to do your shipping. Some find it helpful to do it in the morning, others like to ship as they get orders throughout the day and still others do a combination of both methods. With eBay, you can't create a scan sheet if you ship throughout the day.

If you use shipping software instead of the eBay shipping offered, customers will be more likely to leave positive feedback because their item ships immediately and arrives at their door early. ShippingEasy has a thirty-day free trial, if you're unsure about using the software give it a try before you buy. If you're still not sure... research other shipping software options. Some others that come up in a Google search are ShipStation, Agile Network and ShipWorks. There are many more, find one that fits for you!

Listing

Should you ever try to search your inventory through eBay Seller Hub, you'll find that the search function is borderline dreadful. You have to be exact in your title search, you can't abbreviate. However, if you use listing software like inkFrog, you'll find the search function is much more conducive for quick inventory searches. Listing software also makes relisting super easy! You can setup your items to automatically relist if it goes unsold with no limits on how many times you have it relist! Unlike eBay. eBay has a limit to their automatic relists. Now, which sounds better to you? Unlimited or limited? Definitely the unlimited, right? Go check out listing software and find something that's right for you. A caveat, listing software shouldn't create your listings for you. If you're selling liquidation items where you're creating a listing for one item at a time it will be very time consuming. They are great, however if you're creating a listing with a large quantity.

Here's a tidbit about inkFrog. They offer four versions of the software: free, basic, professional, and unlimited. Give the free version a go and decide for yourself.

Tips and Tricks

RSS Feeds

What is RSS?

RSS stands for "Really Simple Syndication."

RSS is a standardized programming format. It is commonly used for syndicating news headlines so they can be easily distributed to a wide audience.

Personal web-logs are written in RSS format and many webmasters use RSS feeds to provide fresh content to their web sites without having to manually update it. Almost any type of information can be reformatted and distributed via RSS.

So how do you use it?

In order to access an RSS feed, you need an RSS aggregator. Sometimes referred to as an RSS Channel or RSS Reader. (For clarity, the term RSS Reader will be used.)

An RSS Reader automatically checks multiple RSS feeds for new items on an ongoing basis. The reader will notify you of any updated information without the need to visit the web sites to see if there is any new content.

Some browsers allow adding RSS feeds directly to a personal toolbar and some Readers are integrated into email programs, while others run as a standalone program on your computer.

There are many free, standalone RSS readers available on the web.

Once you have downloaded and installed a Reader, you need to subscribe to an RSS feed. This is simply a matter of copying the web address (URL) of the feed into the reader. That's it, the reader does the rest. Anytime any information gets updated the Reader will notify you. The RSS reader we use makes a doorbell sound and pops up a small window whenever our feed or any feeds subscribed to get updated. Make sure whatever Reader you use is capable of understanding RSS version 2.0.

How can Sellers benefit from eBay RSS Listing Feeds?

A feature on eBay allows you get your listings in RSS format. If you have an eBay store you can use the feed to inform your buyers of any new or updated store inventory, auction or buy it now listings and it will also notify you when "Good till Canceled" store inventory is automatically re-listed.

From the bottom of your Store's Home Page or from "Selling Manager", click the "Manage My Store" link. In the left navigation menu under "Store Marketing" click the link labeled "Listing Feeds".

Enable the radio button titled "Distribute your listings via RSS". Optionally enable the radio button titled "Make a file of your Store inventory listings available". Click the "Apply" button to save the changes. It can take up to 12 hours for the listing to be created.

Eventually you will see an orange RSS icon on the bottom left of your store's home page.

How can Buyers benefit from eBay RSS Listing Feeds?

If you're an eBay buyer you can subscribe to your favorite store's RSS feeds. Whenever you see the orange icon on the bottom of a store's home page or any site for that matter, just click on it and then copy the full URL from your address bar into your RSS Reader. You will also see the raw XML code that the feed is programmed in.

You can also right mouse-click on the icon and select "copy" and then paste the URL into your RSS Reader. You Reader will monitor any changes to whatever feeds you subscribe to and notify you.[2]

The main purpose for RSS feeds under tips and tricks is that you can submit your RSS feed to Google, just Google "submit Google URL" and it will pop up a place to a URL and that URL will then be indexed in google search results. Add your RSS URL to your eBay store and now all of your items will populate in google searches for your particular items.

---

[2] http://www.ebay.com/gds/eBay-RSS-FEEDS-FOR-SELLERS-AND-BUYERS-/10000000000756357/g.html *(from Jan 2016)*

Good luck and happy eBaying!

Works Consulted

Business News Daily http://www.businessnewsdaily.com/7543-best-accounting-software.html

Laundry Bag Store Online via eBay http://www.ebay.com/gds/eBay-RSS-FEEDS-FOR-SELLERS-AND-BUYERS-/10000000000756357/g.html (from Jan 2016)

eBay http://www.ebay.com

PayPal http://www.paypal.com

American Pickers http://www.history.com/shows/american-pickers

All screenshots are property of the author.

Printed in Great Britain
by Amazon